31 DAYS OF GRATITUDE

31 DAYS OF GRATITUDE

CREATE THE LIFE YOU DESIRE

Shilamida

ISBN: 1548825891
ISBN-13: 9781548825898

This book is dedicated to those who are looking to live the life they desire! This life we live is hard and trying at times, but when we learn to use the beautiful tools within this journal, life becomes amazingly different.

This work is also dedicated to my firstborn (who is the reason I went down this path); to all of my children; and to the best lover, friend, and partner anyone could ever have. This journal is a commitment of my love to humanity and making this world a better place to live.

Thank you for being a part of my journey.

Shilamida

Be the change that you wish to see in the world.
—Gandhi

My spiritual journey began by looking at this quote daily back in 2008. Wanting to be the best version of me is what I strive for daily. When I am not, I quickly recognize it, apologize, forgive, and keep moving on. Be the best you can be—be the change you wish to see—and life becomes more peaceful. Only we can control how we will affect our existence.

ACKNOWLEDGMENTS

I am forever grateful for the path I have chosen and the signs and messages I have received in order to live it.

I could not have done this without finding Kabbalah first and then *The Secret*, the Law of Attraction, the Americana Leadership College, Deepak Chopra, Wayne Dyer, Louise Hay, the Four Agreements, Buddha, Lao Tzu, Oprah, Gabrielle Bernstein, and all of the healers with whom I have been privileged to work. It was the teachings of these great people and studies that have led me to who I am now.

I am so grateful for my lover, Benjamin, and for all of our children. The unconditional love I have received is big enough to accomplish anything in this world. I am grateful they chose me and have allowed me to become the best version of myself in order to serve anyone in need.

Thank you to all the people who help to make my world go round. It truly takes a village, and I am grateful for mine.

PREFACE

HERE IS THE headspace you need to come to terms with:

You are exactly where you are supposed to be right now. The things you are living through—good or bad—are the reality you've created for yourself. You need to be grateful for every second of that reality. Thank the universe right now for bringing you this experience. This experience is going to make you grow. There will be a time a year from now, five years from now, or ten years from now when this moment will be a faint memory. Find gratitude in the darkest of places.

You must change your negative thoughts by focusing on what you want and being grateful for what you have and what you don't have as though you already possess it. Recognizing your negative thoughts is half of the battle. Once you realize what you are doing, you will be able to change the course of your life. Ask the universe to bring you what you desire. Think about your perfect life. *Stop* focusing on what you don't want. *Stop* focusing on being ill, being heartbroken, and being sad. Focus on what you want! If you don't know what you want, neither does the universe, and you will only get what you are living through now.

You have to find gratitude in everything, and you have to *DREAM BIG*. In order for all this to happen, you have to try to be the best version of you every single day. You can do this. Reread this. Let it sink in. Focus on what you want. Be a good human being. Wake up every morning and decide, "I am going to be the best me I can be today!" When you are not, recognize it, apologize, and forgive.

We are in this together! We are all connected. I am sending you so much love and healing. I wish you the best on your journey, and I know my life's work will help you if you are committed.

xoxo,
Shilamida

INTRODUCTION

YOU ARE ABOUT to thank yourself for opening this book. This is the book that is going to change your entire life! The pages that follow are going to be seeds that you will be planting in order to create the life your soul longs to live. These pages are full of gratitude affirmations that will help you to retrain your thought process in attracting abundance into your life. Please be patient. The process takes time. You are in your current situation because of years and years of stuff that has piled up, so take the time to work on yourself in order for things to change.

Everything in our life is a creation of thought. Every single thing around us started as a thought in someone's mind that became a reality through vision and feeling. Once you start to understand this, you will learn how powerful your thoughts are, whether good, bad, or joking. That's right, even your jokes and sarcasm have power! You will learn how to control that thought process so it works for your greater good.

What does it mean? Manifesting is a way of thinking that summons a thought to action or reality. When you want something, you are coming from a place of ego. The ego drives our wants and desires. When we are trying to manifest, we want to make sure we are coming from a place of love and gratitude.

Wanting and receiving cannot go hand in hand without love and gratitude.

This is why I created the journal you are reading. It is said that it takes twenty-one days to break or form a habit. It took me years to really get into the habit of gratitude. The reality is that gratitude should be a daily practice…one that should never end. If you are grateful every single day, your life will be incredible! You will change as a human being. You will be illuminated. The people around you will also start to change because it will be contagious. You will stop reacting to every little thing that happens and learn how to let things go. You will take the worst of moments and turn them into positive ones.

My Spiritual Rules:

A lot of times, my patients or friends will tell me, "I am trying this gratitude stuff, but nothing is happening. What gives?" Well, it's not as simple as just being grateful. There are laws of nature, laws of attraction, and laws of reflection that come into play with manifesting. You have to understand the laws before you can understand how it all works. You also have to work on yourself spiritually.

These are the ten spiritual rules I try to live by and you should too, before you see results:

1. Recognize the Ego—The Ego self and your higher self are two different people. At any point you can lower the Ego and live from a place of love and light. It is OK to change.

2. Stop Reacting—I used to be a really angry, confrontational person. I would react before I could think. I would have tunnel vision. Instead, I learned how to breathe. I learned there might be another side of the story. I learned to hug instead of yelling.

3. Lead with Love and Blessings—All day every day, as much as you can remember, send people love and blessings. This act alone will change your whole life.

4. Forgive—This is a biggie! If you are harboring a grudge, resentment, or ill feelings, you will have a hard time manifesting. Forgiveness is key. You are only hurting yourself when you don't.

5. I AM" Affirmations—Value yourself! Whatever you put after "I AM *is*! "I am beautiful. I am strong. I am brave. I am love. I am light. I am living my purpose. I am…"

6. Positive thoughts have to outnumber negative thoughts. On any given day, you should have more positive thoughts than negative. Recognize the negative, and replace it with gratitude.

7. Stop Judging and Complaining—Judgment is killer. When you judge someone, you open yourself up for judgment. When you criticize or base an opinion on your own limited view, you are really talking about yourself! What we say reflects what we feel inside.

8. I *CAN*!—No matter what life throws at you from this moment forward, your response to it should always be "I *can*." Remove the word *can't* from your vocabulary. Be conscious in using the word *can*.

9. ASK the Universe—It all starts by asking for what you desire. Do you desire a new career, new love, a safe place,

a healing space? Whatever you need, ask for it. Then be grateful for your life. You *deserve* happiness. You deserve abundance.

10. Believe! — I listed this last so that you can understand the other spiritual rules first. However, it all starts with believing in something greater than what you already know.

The key is to start recognizing your negative thoughts and changing them into positives. *Stop* complaining. This is very important! Next time you feel yourself about to complain, stop yourself, take a look at the situation, and find gratitude instead. For instance, you go to a restaurant and your food comes out cold. Before calling your waiter, be grateful you are in a restaurant, be grateful you have money to pay for this food, be grateful you live in an area where you are free to eat whatever you want, or be grateful you have a roof over your head or that the weather is so nice you get to sit outside. After you've found gratitude in the moment, then you can ask the waiter, in your kindest voice, to please heat up your food. Are you ready to receive? Breathe...

GUIDELINES FOR USING THIS JOURNAL

ON THE PAGES that follow, there are sample gratitude affirmations that work for everyone and empty lines where you can make the process authentic to you. Each day, you want to be grateful for at least twenty things that are in your life right now! You will write those on the sample gratitude-affirmation pages (pages that are on the left). Then add what you want on the blank pages—what your manifestations are, as though you already have them (on the right).

You have to add things you want as if you already have them. Make sure to use these words: "I am grateful for…" Feel the gratitude. Envision the things you want as though you already have them.

After the thirty-one days, there are bonus pages for love, money, and career.

Enjoy the process. Listen. Grow. Shine your light.
The world is waiting.
Thank you for allowing me to guide you.

Warning: Be careful what you wish for. Just like in every great genie movie, wishes always come with a price. In manifesting, wishes come with spiritual lessons. The greater the reward, the greater the healing and the deeper the spiritual work. Be specific in what you want. That is the key. Be conscious of your thoughts and potential self-sabotage.

DAY 1

IMAGINE WHAT LIFE would be like if you said the following words every day. Take a deep breath in through your nose and release. Inhale, release. Inhale, release. On the page provided for you, write the things you are grateful for and then repeat the affirmations. If you are ever in a place where you can't find gratitude, come back to Day 1 and repeat.

I am grateful for strength.
I am grateful for willpower.
I am grateful for discipline.
I am grateful for messages.
I am open to receiving.
I am grateful I can hear with an open mind.
I am grateful for love.
I am grateful for calm.
I am grateful for peace.
I am grateful for forgiveness.
I am grateful for compassion.
I am grateful for kindness.
I am grateful for connections.
I am grateful for support.
I am grateful for truth.
I am grateful for breath.
I am grateful for hope.
I am grateful for fun.
I am grateful for dancing.
I am grateful for gratitude.

Happiness is a choice. Choose to be happy now!

I am grateful for…

_____

_____

_____

_____

_____

_____

_____

_____

_____

_____

_____

_____

_____

_____

_____

_____

_____

_____

_____

_____

_____

_____

_____

_____

_____

DAY 2

BE GRATEFUL NOW! Repeat the gratitude statements below, and add your gratitude statements afterward. Find things to be grateful for right now, no matter what stage of life you are in. Remember, if you are manifesting, you have to manifest in the present, as if you already have what you want. Like attracts like. Use the present tense.

I am grateful for breath.
I am grateful for fresh air.
I am grateful for life.
I am grateful for today.
I am grateful for my eyes and the ability to see.
I am grateful for messages.
I am grateful I am listening.
I am grateful I am open.
I am grateful for guidance.
I am grateful for love.
I am grateful for opportunity.
I am grateful for manifesting.
I am grateful for knowledge.
I am grateful for hope.
I am grateful for faith.
I am grateful for strength.
I am grateful for peace.
I am grateful for calm.
I am grateful for willpower.
I am grateful for the ability to heal myself.

I am grateful for _____

_____

_____

_____

_____

_____

_____

_____

_____

_____

_____

_____

_____

_____

_____

_____

_____

_____

_____

_____

_____

_____

_____

_____

_____

_____

_____

I am love. I am light. I am strong.

DAY 3

———————— ⌢ ————————

TODAY I WANT you to focus on your breathing. Most of us hold our breaths. If that's you…*breathe. Inhale…two…three…exhale…two… three.* You would be surprised to see how breathing can help you in any given situation. Yoga has allowed me to connect my body, mind, and spirit. Find a way to move and breathe that serves you. You won't regret it. Come back here often.

I am grateful for breath.
I am grateful for inhaling.
I am grateful for exhaling.
I am grateful for fresh air.
I am grateful for oxygen.
I am grateful for the human body.
I am grateful for working, healthy lungs.
I am grateful for my good health.
I am grateful for living.
I am grateful for relaxation.
I am grateful for _____
I am grateful for _____
I am grateful for _____
I am grateful for _____
I am grateful for _____
I am grateful for _____
I am grateful for _____
I am grateful for _____

Thank you for fulfilling my every desire.
Thank you for guiding me.
Thank you for every single day I get to live this beautiful life.
I am grateful for every experience.
Thank you for enlightening me.
Thank you for awareness.
Thank you for responsibility.
Thank you for accountability.
Thank you for today, and thank you for an amazing tomorrow!

_____
_____
_____
_____
_____
_____
_____
_____
_____
_____
_____
_____
_____
_____
_____
_____
_____

DAY 4

START WITH YOUR gratitude. Look around the room. There are so many things to be grateful for. Everything around you see was created by a thought. Your thoughts are power. Feel inside what you really want. What are you grateful for?

I am grateful for _____

I am grateful for _____

I am grateful for _____

I am grateful for _____

I am grateful for _____

I am grateful for _____

I am grateful for _____

I am grateful for _____

I am grateful for _____

I am grateful for _____

I am grateful for _____

I am grateful for _____

I am grateful for _____

I am grateful for _____

I am grateful for _____

I am grateful for _____

I am grateful for _____

I am grateful for _____

I am grateful for _____

Thank you, universe, for always providing for me.

I am grateful for _____

I am grateful for _____

I am grateful for _____

I am grateful for _____

I am grateful for _____

I am grateful for _____

I am grateful for _____

I am grateful for _____

_____

_____

_____

_____

_____

_____

_____

_____

_____

_____

_____

_____

_____

_____

_____

_____

_____

_____

_____

_____

DAY 5

If you are just tuning in, find things in your life to be grateful for right now! If you are in a bad place, dig deep, and look around you. Even if you feel your life is not at its potential, there are things to be grateful for. I am grateful for heat. I am grateful for the Internet. I am grateful for running water. We take things for granted every single day. Find some gratitude and then make a mantra about what you are grateful for. This will shift the energy in your life.

I am grateful for messages.
I am grateful I am open.
I am grateful I am listening.
I am grateful I am conscious.
I am grateful I am aware.
I am grateful for guidance.
I am grateful for protection.
I am grateful for safety.
I am grateful for faith.
I am grateful for love.
I am grateful for every moment.
I am grateful for _____
I am grateful for _____
I am grateful for _____
I am grateful for _____
I am grateful for _____
I am grateful for _____
I am grateful for _____

I am grateful for _____

I am grateful for _____

I am grateful for _____

_____

_____

_____

_____

_____

_____

_____

_____

_____

_____

_____

_____

_____

_____

_____

_____

_____

_____

_____

_____

_____

Repeat this Mantra:
I am safe. I am OK. I am protected.
I am safe. I am OK. I am protected.
I am safe. I am OK. I am protected

DAY 6

⟡

INTENTION IS HOW we acquire what we want. If you set the intention of your day the night before, as you awake in the morning, you will see a drastic change in yourself, and the behavior of those around you.

Today is going to be an amazing day.
Today is a new day.
Today is the day when all the possibilities of life are available to me.
I am grateful I am alive.
I am grateful I slept in a bed last night.
I am grateful for clean sheets.
I am grateful for clean water.
I am grateful for fresh air.
I am grateful for a beautiful day.
I am grateful for smiling faces.
I am grateful for laughter.
I am grateful for gentle encounters.
I am grateful for my true calling in life.
I am grateful I find my way always.
I am grateful for opportunities.
I am grateful that every phone call, text message, and e-mail today is a good one filled with love and peace.
I am grateful for _____
I am grateful for _____
I am grateful for _____
I am grateful for _____

What is it that you Desire? Be grateful for it, like you already have it!

I am grateful for _____

I am grateful for _____

I am grateful for _____

I am grateful for _____

_____

_____

_____

_____

_____

_____

_____

_____

_____

_____

_____

_____

_____

_____

_____

_____

_____

_____

_____

_____

_____

DAY 7

WHEN YOU ARE being grateful, make sure you are feeling the energy of the gratitude. If the list you are reading does not resonate with you, make it your own. Close your eyes and feel. Similar to the butterfly feeling of falling in love, feel it in your gut. Love yourself, brethe and repeat:

I am grateful for life.
I am grateful for love.
I am grateful for hope.
I am grateful for faith.
I am grateful for peace.
I am grateful for calm.
I am grateful for healing.
I am grateful for healers.
I am grateful I am focused.
I am grateful for time management.
I am grateful for food.
I am grateful for water.
I am grateful I am present.
I am grateful for smiles.
I am grateful for hugs.
I am grateful for kisses.
I am grateful for breath.
I am grateful for laughter.
I am grateful money flows through me easily.
I am grateful for fun.

Value yourself—no matter where you are in life right now.
You are special!

I am grateful for _____

_____

_____

_____

_____

_____

_____

_____

_____

_____

_____

_____

_____

_____

_____

_____

_____

_____

_____

_____

When you undervalue what you do, the
world will undervalue who you are.
—Oprah Winfrey

DAY 8

IN EVERY GIVEN moment, there is gratitude to be found. In the very worst moments is when it is most important to find gratitude. Remember, it is a practice. It does not just come naturally, so don't get discouraged. Keep at it, and you will see a change.

I am grateful for _____
I am grateful for _____
I am grateful for _____
I am grateful for _____
I am grateful for _____
I am grateful for _____
I am grateful for _____
I am grateful for _____
I am grateful for _____
I am grateful for _____
I am grateful for _____
I am grateful for _____
I am grateful for _____
I am grateful for _____
I am grateful for _____
I am grateful for _____
I am grateful for _____
I am grateful for _____
I am grateful for _____
I am grateful for _____

_____

_____

_____
_____
_____
_____
_____
_____
_____
_____
_____
_____
_____
_____
_____
_____
_____
_____
_____
_____
_____
_____
_____
_____

Oh thank you Universe. Thank you, thank you, thank you! Thank you for downtime. Thank you for time to unwind. Thank you for rest. Thank you for healing. Thank you for knowledge. Thank you for learning. Thank you for listening. Thank you for messages. Thank you for kindness. Thank you for love. Thank you for guidance. Thank you for time. Thank you for healing. Thank you for everything!

DAY 9

DO YOU BELIEVE? You have to believe in order to receive. Today I want you to make sure to add in on the lines provided, something you want that you do not have, but to act as though you already have it. It could be something simple like a great parking spot at the grocery store or a phone call from a friend you miss. Feel it, really feel it, and believe it will happen.

I am grateful for this beautiful life I've created.
I am grateful for the obstacles that have led me to this moment.
I am grateful for the obstacles I still have to live through.
I am grateful for peace.
I am grateful for love.
I am grateful I lead with love and compassion always.
I am grateful for learning.
I am grateful for understanding.
I am grateful I am listening.
I am grateful for my life!
I am grateful for _____
I am grateful for _____
I am grateful for _____
I am grateful for _____
I am grateful for _____
I am grateful for _____
I am grateful for _____
I am grateful for _____
I am grateful for _____

I am grateful for _____

_____

_____

_____

_____

_____

_____

_____

_____

_____

_____

_____

_____

_____

_____

_____

_____

_____

_____

_____

_____

_____

_____

_____

I can overcome anything.
I am strong.
*I am **enough**!*
I BELIEVE!

DAY 10

LIFE IS WHAT we make of it. We are the creators of our destiny. If you want it, *you can* have it! Everything you want is in your reach. Just ask and believe. Thank you, universe, for always providing me with challenges I can overcome. Thank you, universe, for calm. Thank you for peace. Thank you for strength. Thank you for health. Thank you for making me stronger.

I am grateful for _____

I am grateful for _____

I am grateful for _____

I am grateful for _____

I am grateful for _____

I am grateful for _____

I am grateful for _____

I am grateful for _____

I am grateful for _____

I am grateful for _____

I am grateful for _____

I am grateful for _____

I am grateful for _____

I am grateful for _____

I am grateful for _____

I am grateful for _____

I am grateful for _____

I am grateful for _____

I am grateful for _____

I am grateful for _____

I am grateful for _____

I am grateful for _____

I am grateful for _____

_____

_____

_____

_____

_____

_____

_____

_____

_____

_____

_____

_____

_____

_____

_____

_____

_____

_____

_____

_____

*Be the best person you can be every single moment of the
day. When you are not, apologize, forgive, and repeat.*

DAY 11

Now that you are getting into the habit of gratitude, let's really do some work! Are you living your life's purpose? Are you feeling sad, anxious, or depressed? This is a great page of gratitude and affirmations to help you calm your mind and body and to help you connect to your soul's purpose.

I am grateful! I am grateful! I am grateful!
I am grateful right now!
I am happy.
I am safe.
I am loved.
I am protected.
I am grateful for my life's purpose.
I am grateful for change.
I am grateful for growth.
I am grateful for spirituality.
I am grateful for knowledge.
I am grateful for listening.
I am grateful for this life.
I am the best me I can be! I am love. I am light!
I am grateful for _____
I am grateful for _____
I am grateful for _____
I am grateful for _____
I am grateful for _____
I am grateful for _____
I am grateful for _____

I am grateful for _____

I am grateful for _____

I am grateful for _____

I am grateful for _____

_____

_____

_____

_____

_____

_____

_____

_____

_____

_____

_____

_____

_____

_____

_____

_____

_____

_____

_____

_____

_____

When we fulfill our function, which is to truly love ourselves and share love with others, then true happiness sets in.
—Gabrielle Bernstein

DAY 12

LOVE IS AN important piece of the puzzle. Are you sending enough love into the world? Are you loving yourself? If you are working on this journal and not seeing a change, you need to send love. Send love to all the people you encounter today; send them love in your mind. Stand in front of the mirror and say to yourself "I love you" over and over again until you feel it and mean it. It's a tough one, but you can do it! And if you are angry with someone, send them the most love. Trust me.

I am grateful for love.
I am grateful for sharing.
I am grateful for feeling.
I am grateful for emotion.
I am grateful for communication.
I am grateful for trust.
I am grateful for honesty.
I am grateful for connections.
I am grateful for healthy relationships.
I am grateful for support.
I am grateful for guidance.
I am grateful for unconditional love.
I am grateful for emotional stability.
I am grateful for passion.
I am grateful for devotion.
I am grateful for _____
I am grateful for _____
I am grateful for _____
I am grateful for _____

Love is the great miracle cure. Loving ourselves works miracles in our lives.
—Louise Hay

DAY 13

TODAY IS A new day! Right now is a chance for a fresh start! Take a few deep breaths. Set a positive intention for today, and be grateful.

I am grateful today is going to be an amazing day.
I am grateful all of my encounters are peaceful.
I am grateful I can help everyone I encounter with a smile.
I am grateful for today.
I am grateful I speak the right words with everyone I meet.
I am grateful I lead with a kind heart.
I am grateful I am patient with the world.
I am grateful for change.
I am grateful for love.
I am grateful for _____
I am grateful for _____
I am grateful for _____
I am grateful for _____
I am grateful for _____
I am grateful for _____
I am grateful for _____
I am grateful for _____
I am grateful for _____
I am grateful for _____

_____
_____
_____
_____
_____

I am the creator of my own miracles; I am the master of my thoughts…I am that, I am.
—Wayne Dyer

The *I AM* statement is beyond powerful. Whatever you put behind it trains your brain to believe it. "I am beautiful. I am strong. I am power. I am light."

What are you? Use this page to affirm it to yourself and the world!

I *AM* _____

I AM _____

I AM _____

I AM _____

I AM _____

I AM _____

I AM _____

I AM _____

I AM _____

I AM _____

I AM _____

I AM _____

I AM _____

I AM _____

I AM _____

I AM _____

I AM _____

I AM _____

I AM _____

DAY 14

ARE YOU WORRIED about money? Is financial stability what you are seeking? The most important lesson I've learned along the way about money is that the more you worry about it, the more money problems you will have. Money is energy, just like anything else. It is meant to move and flow just like any other energy. When we hold on to and hoard it, we are creating a block in moving energy. Stop worrying about money, and focus on having all the money you need. If you are experiencing a lot of unforeseen issues like parking tickets, flat tires, and broken house parts, it's because you are not giving and sharing enough. Next time the cashier asks you at a checkout counter to donate one dollar, do it! Next time you pull up to a light and there are can shakers, *give*—even if you don't have the money to spare. When you give, you summon the universe to return.

I am grateful for abundance.
I am grateful for unlimited income.
I am grateful the universe provides me with everything I need.
I am grateful I am always taken care of.
I am grateful I have enough.
I am grateful I *AM ENOUGH.*
I am grateful my budget is unlimited.
I am grateful for $_____ a week.
I am grateful money flows through me.
I am grateful I can help others whenever I can.
I am grateful for financial stability.

I am grateful for _____
I am grateful for _____
I am grateful for _____
I am grateful for _____
I am grateful for _____
I am grateful for _____
I am grateful for _____
I am grateful for _____
I am grateful for _____
I am grateful for _____

_____
_____
_____
_____
_____
_____
_____
_____
_____
_____
_____
_____
_____
_____

Money flows through me. I always have more than enough.
I am abundant.

DAY 15

FEAR. ANXIETY. DEPRESSION. They are all learned behaviors that are holding you back. You can control these feelings. What we think, we create. If you have a lot of fear, stop watching the news, mystery shows, or cop dramas. Cut yourself off from imagination, and live in the here and now. Repeat over and over: *I am OK. I am safe. I am love. I am light.*

I am grateful for security.
I am grateful for safety.
I am grateful for love.
I am grateful for trust.
I am grateful I am OK.
I am grateful I am at peace.
I am grateful for calm.
I am grateful I am breathing.
I am grateful for protection.
I am grateful for guidance.
I am grateful for _____
I am grateful for _____
I am grateful for _____
I am grateful for _____
I am grateful for _____
I am grateful for _____
I am grateful for _____
I am grateful for _____
I am grateful for _____
I am grateful for _____

_____
_____
_____
_____
_____
_____
_____
_____
_____
_____
_____
_____
_____
_____
_____
_____
_____
_____
_____
_____
_____
_____
_____
_____
_____

I am protected. I live in light. I am surrounded with white light and love.
I am OK…I am OK…I am OK.

DAY 16

THE EGO IS that little voice inside our heads trying to convince us to go against our gut instinct. You have to learn to recognize this voice and to fight it. That feeling in your stomach is what you have to tune in to.

I am grateful I recognize my ego and do not react to it.
I am grateful I am connected to my instinct.
I am grateful I always know the right thing to do for me.
I am grateful I always speak the right words.
I am grateful I am open.
I am grateful I am aware.
I am grateful for opportunities to grow.
I am grateful I am learning every day.
I am grateful I am safe.
I am grateful I am protected.
I am grateful for _____
I am grateful for _____
I am grateful for _____
I am grateful for _____
I am grateful for _____
I am grateful for _____
I am grateful for _____
I am grateful for _____
I am grateful for _____

_____
_____
_____

_____
_____
_____
_____
_____
_____
_____
_____
_____
_____
_____
_____
_____
_____
_____
_____
_____
_____
_____
_____
_____
_____
_____
_____

Take a deep breath in. Exhale. Breathe in.
Ask the universe for what you want. Be spe-
cific…Now, be patient and take action!

DAY 17

ALONG MY JOURNEY, I have realized that the natural world around us is so beautiful. The trees, the stars, the flowers, the rain—it's all alive. All of these things are going through their own life cycle of growth. Find a piece of nature to connect with today. For me, my favorite is the ocean. I love to manifest traveling and have seen some of the most beautiful places because of it. What part of nature serves you? Be grateful for it now, and if you want to travel, here's how I manifest it:

I am grateful for the ocean.
I am grateful for the sand.
I am grateful for calm waters.
I am grateful for sunshine.
I am grateful for the smell of saltwater.
I am grateful I always sleep in a comfortable place.
I am grateful for beautiful beaches.
I am grateful I fly with ease.
I am grateful for new experiences.
I am grateful for fun.
I am grateful for discovery.
I am grateful for _____
I am grateful for _____
I am grateful for _____
I am grateful for _____
I am grateful for _____
I am grateful for _____
I am grateful for _____

I am grateful for _____

I am grateful for _____

I am grateful for _____

_____

_____

_____

_____

_____

_____

_____

_____

_____

_____

_____

_____

_____

_____

_____

_____

_____

_____

_____

Be thankful for what you have; you'll end up having more. If you concentrate on what you don't have, you will never, ever have enough.
—Oprah Winfrey

DAY 18

WE TAKE SO much for granted around us. Now that you are well on your way into a spiritual life, don't forget about the little things around you. There are so many people in this world without food, without clean water, and without a place to live. Be grateful for all the small things in life. (If you are reading this and don't have the things below, be grateful first for the things in your life, and then use this as a manifesting list.)

I am grateful for delicious foods.
I am grateful for clean running water.
I am grateful for clean drinking water.
I am grateful for nutritious foods.
I am grateful for electricity.
I am grateful for a working air conditioner everywhere I go.
I am grateful for heat when it is cold everywhere I go.
I am grateful for clean clothes.
I am grateful for a washer and dryer that clean my clothes.
I am grateful for writing utensils that work.
I am grateful for my working smartphone.
I am grateful for transportation.
I am grateful for clean sheets.
I am grateful for clean air.
I am grateful for working Wi-Fi.
I am grateful for _____
I am grateful for _____
I am grateful for _____
I am grateful for _____

I am grateful for _____
I am grateful for _____
I am grateful for _____
I am grateful for _____
I am grateful for _____
I am grateful for _____

DAY 19

———

ALONG THIS JOURNEY you will be faced with tough times. It is all a test. Do not get sucked in. Use the tools you are learning about to overcome what you are facing. If you do, you will grow. If you don't, you will relive it over and over again.

I am grateful for happiness.
I am grateful for life.
I am grateful I am right where I belong.
I am grateful I am living my life's purpose.
I am grateful for my path.
I am grateful for this journey.
I am grateful I am open.
I am grateful for messages.
I am grateful for love.
I am grateful for faith.
I am grateful for hope.
I am grateful for healing.
I am grateful I am listening to the messages I receive.
I am grateful I am protected.
I am grateful I am calm.
I am grateful I am surrounded by calm.
I am grateful for _____
I am grateful for _____
I am grateful for _____
I am grateful for _____
I am grateful for _____

Don't be afraid. Your journey is just beginning.
Amazing things are on their way. Feel that energy.

DAY 20

A BIG PART of this journey is realizing who is in your life for a reason, whether it be for a season or a lifetime. Just because they are called family or you have been friends for life does not mean these people serve you. Today, be grateful for what you have, and then summon the energy to bring loving, supportive relationships to you.

I am grateful for life.
I am grateful for love.
I am grateful for protection.
I am grateful for safety.
I am grateful for true friendships.
I am grateful for support.
I am grateful for truth.
I am grateful for trust.
I am grateful I am surrounded by love and support.
I am grateful I inspire others to be better.
I am grateful I work on myself every single day.
I am grateful for growth.
I am grateful for awareness.
I am grateful for believing.
I am grateful for gratitude.
I am grateful for _____
I am grateful for _____
I am grateful for _____
I am grateful for _____
I am grateful for _____

**What other people think of you
is none of your business**.
—Unknown
—Credit to JT Foxx for teaching this to me

_____
_____
_____
_____
_____
_____
_____
_____
_____
_____
_____
_____
_____
_____
_____
_____
_____
_____
_____
_____

Don't let the judgment of others stand in your way
on this journey. At this point you are contagious and
sharing your light and knowledge. Negative people
around you will start to leave you. It's OK. Let go.

DAY 21

———

WE DESERVE TO live a life of happiness. We deserve all the good things in life as well. If you have been conditioned to fear money or success, let that go! You deserve anything you want!

I am worthy.
I deserve everything good life has to offer.
I am enough.
I am grateful for all the things I desire.
I am grateful I do not stand in the way of my happiness.
I am grateful for laughter.
I am grateful for joy.
I am grateful for unlimited income.
I am grateful for riches.
I am grateful for abundance.
I am grateful for a new car.
I am grateful for a new house.
I am grateful for a new boat.
I am grateful for _____
I am grateful for _____
I am grateful for _____
I am grateful for _____
I am grateful for _____
I am grateful for _____
I am grateful for _____
I am grateful for _____
I am grateful for _____
I am grateful for _____

---

*We have been conditioned to have fearful or bad feel-
ings about money. We need to let those go and em-
brace that we deserve anything our hearts desire.
What kind of luxury do you desire? It's OK.*

DAY 22

Congratulations! If you have been working on this journal for the last twenty-one days, you have officially made it a habit. Great work! I am *so* proud of you! And you should be proud of yourself. You should be seeing a shift in energy now. If you are not, then you still have a lot of spiritual work to do in the departments of love and forgiveness. If you are starting to manifest, I give you this warning: be careful what you wish for! As you start to grow, you will start getting *everything* you ask for *and* everything you think of. So watch your thoughts. You are *always* creating.

I am grateful for love.
I am grateful I love myself.
I am grateful for forgiveness.
I am grateful I forgive myself.
I am grateful my thoughts become reality.
I am grateful I can learn and grow with little suffering.
I am grateful I have the tools to overcome anything and everything.
I am grateful the messages are clear around me.
I am grateful I am listening.
I am grateful I am specific in asking the universe for what I want.
I am grateful I am sharing my gift with others.
I am grateful I am an inspiration.
I am grateful for _____
I am grateful for _____
I am grateful for _____
I am grateful for _____
I am grateful for _____
I am grateful for _____

Dream and follow your heart.
What do you desire?

_____
_____
_____
_____
_____
_____
_____
_____
_____
_____
_____
_____
_____
_____
_____
_____
_____
_____
_____
_____
_____
_____
_____
_____
_____
_____
_____
_____

DAY 23

—◦—

You now have the power and the tools to create every portion of your life. Use them wisely, and don't slack off. If bad things start to happen, be grateful! Don't forget the practice. It is a discipline.

I am grateful for today.
I am grateful for my lover.
I am grateful for a strong and healthy relationship.
I am grateful we are growing old together in sound mind.
I am grateful we live in peace and harmony.
I am grateful for life.
I am grateful for fun.
I am grateful for travel.
I am grateful for messages.
I am grateful for discipline.
I am grateful for willpower.
I am grateful for strength.
I am grateful for my desires.
I am grateful for passion.
I am grateful for _____
I am grateful for _____
I am grateful for _____
I am grateful for _____
I am grateful for _____

With Gratitude I Ask,
Through Gratitude I Believe,
and in Gratitude I Receive...
Whatever my heart desires.
—*The Secret Gratitude Book*[1]

_____

_____

_____

_____

_____

_____

_____

_____

_____

_____

_____

_____

_____

_____

_____

_____

_____

_____

_____

_____

_____

_____

1 Rhonda Byrne, *The Secret Gratitude Book* (New York, NY: Atria Books, 2007), Page 133

DAY 24

FORGIVENESS IS ONE of the greatest lessons of them all. It is time to let go. First you have to learn to forgive yourself. Stand in front of a mirror and tell yourself "I love you...I forgive you" over and over again, until you feel it deep down inside. This is important. Once you forgive yourself, you will be able to forgive others, and more importantly, you will be able to ask for forgiveness. That's powerful stuff!

I am grateful for forgiveness.
I am grateful for the strength to forgive others.
I am grateful for the strength to forgive myself.
I am grateful I love myself.
I am grateful others around me forgive me.
I am grateful for apologies.
I am grateful for peace.
I am grateful for calm.
I am grateful for agreement.
I am grateful for apologies.
I am grateful for acceptance.
I am grateful for understanding.
I am grateful for letting go.
I am grateful for _____
I am grateful for _____
I am grateful for _____
I am grateful for _____
I am grateful for _____
I am grateful for _____

Forgive others, not because they deserve it,
but because you deserve peace.

Use this space to think about situations
where you need to find forgiveness—whether it's forgiving yourself or someone else.

I am sorry. Please forgive me. Thank you, I love you.
—Ho'oponopono

_____

_____

_____

_____

_____

_____

_____

_____

_____

_____

_____

_____

_____

_____

_____

_____

_____

_____

_____

DAY 25

YOU SHOULD *REALLY* be noticing the change by now. All of the effort you are putting forth is resulting in changes in your life at this very moment. Change is scary; it's the unknown. Don't focus on that. Focus on what you want. Be grateful for what you want. You have to change in order to grow and in order to attract what you want. Focus. It's the best advice I can give you.

I am grateful for change.
I am grateful for courage.
I am grateful for strength.
I am grateful for trust.
I am grateful for new experiences.
I am grateful for walking down new paths.
I am grateful for growth.
I am grateful for discipline.
I am grateful for gratitude.
I am grateful for power.
I am grateful for support.
I am grateful for loving relationships.
I am grateful for flow.
I am grateful for breath.
I am grateful for dreams coming true.
I am grateful for vision.
I am grateful for feeling.
I am grateful for _____
I am grateful for _____
I am grateful for _____
I am grateful for _____

I am grateful for _____

_____
_____
_____
_____
_____
_____
_____
_____
_____
_____
_____
_____
_____
_____
_____
_____
_____
_____
_____
_____
_____
_____

What action will you take to complete the thirty- and sixty-
day plans you developed? What kind of help do you need?
Is it supplies, money, love? What do you need? Breathe.
Feel it. Be grateful for it like you already have it.

DAY 26

HAVE YOU BEEN receiving any messages? Are you listening? The messages are all around us—in the numbers we see or in the animals we encounter. We need to be listening, open, and ready to receive. In a blink of an eye, we might miss it. Pay attention. Ask for it. Believe in it.

I am grateful for manifesting.
I am grateful for the Law of Attraction.
I am grateful for messages.
I am grateful for awareness.
I am grateful for connections.
I am grateful for my subconscious mind.
I am grateful for my conscious mind.
I am grateful for dreams.
I am grateful for wishes.
I am grateful for vision.
I am grateful for creation.
I am grateful for imagination.
I am grateful for existence.
I am grateful for energy.
I am grateful for sharing.
I am grateful for knowledge.
I am grateful for _____
I am grateful for _____
I am grateful for _____
I am grateful for _____
I am grateful for _____

You should be *so* proud of yourself! You have been planting all these seeds, and your energy vibration is high. The stuff you are putting out there will come back to you in this lifetime. How quickly things come to you depends on you. Are you sharing financially, emotionally, spiritually? You have to give a lot more than you are receiving. It doesn't have to be money. A smile is sharing—so is holding a door open or letting someone cut in front of you in line.

Use this space to make a list of sharing. Who can you help, inspire, or love? Send text messages sharing love and light. Be nice.

_____
_____
_____
_____
_____
_____
_____
_____
_____
_____
_____
_____
_____
_____
_____
_____
_____

DAY 27

IF YOU DIDN'T believe before, I am hoping you believe now. There is a greater source that we all come from. No matter what your religion, race, or creed…we all came from the same source. Everything around you was created by a thought. Once you put the pieces of this puzzle together, you'll realize how important it is to have spirituality in your life to trust along the way. Be good. Dream big. Envision life. Be grateful. Have hope.

I am grateful for hope.
I am grateful for faith.
I am grateful for belief.
I am grateful for spirituality.
I am grateful for a higher power.
I am grateful for answers.
I am grateful for communication.
I am grateful for learning.
I am grateful for practicing.
I am grateful for _____
I am grateful for _____
I am grateful for _____
I am grateful for _____
I am grateful for _____
I am grateful for _____
I am grateful for _____
I am grateful for _____

Close your eyes. Take a couple of deep breaths. Fill yourself up with light. Feel yourself surrounded in white light. Make a circle of light around you. You are protected. I'm sending you so much love and light.

DAY 28

IF YOU HAVE not started the process yet, it is time to heal now. It is time to heal yourself. We have all lived through a lot. We all have the choice to play the victim or to shine our light. I hope you choose to shine your light. You are an inspiration! You give motivation! Share your knowledge with others.

I am grateful for healing.
I am grateful for growth.
I am grateful for change.
I am grateful for moving forward.
I am grateful for improvement.
I am grateful for strength.
I am grateful I inspire.
I am grateful I can serve others.
I am grateful for opportunities to grow.
I am grateful for peace.
I am grateful for calm.
I am grateful for _____
I am grateful for _____
I am grateful for _____
I am grateful for _____
I am grateful for _____
I am grateful for _____
I am grateful for _____
I am grateful for _____

Heaven on earth is a choice you must make, not a place you must find.
--Wayne Dyer

DAY 29

———— ⌒ ————

Don't ever forget where you came from. Once you realize your source of power and create the life your soul longs to live, do not forget the struggle that got you to this point. Your story can now shift the life of another. Come back to this journal over and over. Don't stop the energy of what brought you here. Keep on doing your great work and *shine your light*.

I am grateful for breath.
I am grateful for life.
I am grateful for air.
I am grateful for a healthy body.
I am grateful for food.
I am grateful for shelter.
I am grateful for water.
I am grateful for love.
I am grateful for my lover.
I am grateful for family.
I am grateful for friends.
I am grateful for happiness.
I am grateful for success.
I am grateful for money.
I am grateful for _____
I am grateful for _____
I am grateful for _____
I am grateful for _____
I am grateful for _____
I am grateful for _____
I am grateful for _____

_____

_____

_____

_____

_____

_____

_____

_____

_____

_____

_____

_____

_____

_____

_____

_____

_____

_____

_____

_____

_____

_____

_____

_____

*Have you figured it out? Have you
mapped out the life you want?
Stay in your momentum!
The life you desire is on its way.*

DAY 30

THANK YOU, THANK you, thank you! Thank you, universe, for introducing me to the Law of Attraction! Thank you for teaching me gratitude. Thank you for giving me the tools and rules of survival. I am forever grateful. Being a student of life and knowledge will better my human existence.

I am grateful for gratitude.
I am grateful for manifesting.
I am grateful for the Law of Attraction.
I am grateful for the universe.
I am grateful for this book.
I am grateful for learning.
I am grateful for knowledge.
I am grateful for applying the tools I have received.
I am grateful for today.
I am grateful for tomorrow.
I am grateful for _____
I am grateful for _____
I am grateful for _____
I am grateful for _____
I am grateful for _____
I am grateful for _____
I am grateful for _____
I am grateful for _____

_____
_____
_____

_____

_____

_____

_____

_____

_____

_____

_____

_____

_____

_____

_____

_____

_____

_____

_____

_____

_____

_____

_____

_____

_____

_____

_____

_____

_____

_____

_____

_____

DAY 31

Go BACK AND reread all the things you are grateful for. Feel the love and energy behind your work. Use this page to create the life your soul longs to live. Anything you desire can be received.

I am grateful for the future.
I am grateful for my dreams coming true.
I am grateful for _____
I am grateful for _____
I am grateful for _____
I am grateful for _____
I am grateful for _____
I am grateful for _____
I am grateful for _____
I am grateful for _____
I am grateful for _____
I am grateful for _____
I am grateful for _____
I am grateful for _____
I am grateful for _____
I am grateful for _____
I am grateful for _____
I am grateful for _____
I am grateful for _____
I am grateful for _____
I am grateful for _____
I am grateful for _____
Congratulations!

Congratulations!!!
You did it!
You have planted the seeds of the life you desire.
Be open, listen, and be ready to do the work.
Don't forget to breathe.

Have more to manifest? Start over! _____

_____
_____
_____
_____
_____
_____
_____
_____
_____
_____
_____
_____
_____
_____
_____
_____
_____
_____
_____
_____
_____
_____
_____

AFTERWORD

THANK YOU, UNIVERSE. Thank you for teaching me this magic. Thank you for giving me this power. Thank you for guiding me to this place where everything I imagine comes true. Thank you for helping me to help others do the same. Thank you for choosing me to share your message. There are signs and messages all around us. These signs and messages will lead us to our true happiness. Are you looking? Are you listening? Are you open to receiving? Be grateful for messages. Be grateful you are open. Be grateful for receiving. *Your words are so powerful.*

Let's be grateful. Stop complaining. Be open. Give every person you see a chance. Forgive. Change your negative thoughts. Be conscious. Stop gossiping. Lift people up even if you think they are not worthy. Stop judging; it'll make your life easier. I promise when you learn how to forgive yourself, you learn to forgive other people. When you realize you have an ego, you can learn how to control it instead of allowing it to control you. Recognize that the things you hate the most in the person you dislike are just qualities inside you that you need to correct and forgive in yourself first. Then you have to learn to forgive everyone else who you believe has wronged you. You see, this is the process. You have to work on yourself spiritually before your manifestations come true.

Ten years ago I lived on Sperber Road dreaming in my bed. I was a single mom, broke, collecting food stamps, and at times hopeless. I started to put the rules into play, and I created my vision board, my gratitude journal, and my dreams. I would dream so big. I would lie in my bed and imagine myself being a really successful entrepreneur—one people looked up to and wanted to do business with. I saw myself as a trophy wife getting picked up by drivers and taken out. I was filled with love even though my world was far from perfect. It took a lot of work. You can do it. Be grateful for your life. Find gratitude in each day. Love. Forgive. Love. Forgive. Grow. Then your dreams will start coming true. I was grateful that I was a healer. I wanted to help people so much. I was grateful for my soul mate as I described him. I dreamed of things that are now all coming true, including being a spiritual guide.

I thank those of you who are paying attention. I'm *so happy* for you! Because if you are being grateful and listening to what I'm saying, your desires are on their way—spiritually, physically, mentally. Once you connect the three and stay in that happy place, your anxiety, sadness, and depression will go away, and your mind and universe connection will explode. Then every physical thing you ask for will come true too. There's actually an art to gratitude. I've figured it out, and I hope I've helped you figure it out, too, if you are open. I'm looking forward to learning more and sharing with you. I hope you find your own true happiness and live the life your soul longs for! If you fall off track, hop back on. It takes practice, discipline, and willpower, but I know you *can* do this!

Namaste,
Shilamida

BONUS PAGES

The following pages are to assist you in manifesting love, money, and purpose. Use the pages that follow at any point in this book.

For more Gratitude Inspiration and Bonus Pages sign up at: Shilamida.com

Don't lose the momentum you've worked so hard to achieve! The key to living your best and most abundant life is consistency and discipline. You've already put in the work for the last 31 days... I can help you keep it up with my Gratitude Membership.
https://shilamida.com/gratitude-membership-become-best-version-you/

And are we friends on social media yet? I am constantly posting lessons and words of wisdom in my various profiles. There's also a FREE supportive community from which you can draw wisdom, motivation and inspiration:www.facebook.com/groups/shilamidainspires
Instagram: https://instagram.com/goddess_of_gratitude
Pinterest: https://www.pinterest.com/Shilamida/
YouTube: https://www.youtube.com/c/GoddessofGratitude
LinkedIn: https://www.linkedin.com/in/shilamida-kupershteyn-9534624/

LOVE

I am grateful for love.
I am grateful for unconditional love.
I am grateful for my soul mate.
I am grateful for my partner who wor-
ships the ground I walk on.
I am grateful I am an amazing partner.
I am grateful for attraction to my partner.
I am grateful for emotional stability.
I am grateful for financial stability.
I am grateful for mental stability.
I am grateful for emotional availability.
I am grateful for a single mate.
I am grateful for romance.
I am grateful for fun.
I am grateful for excitement.
I am grateful for good sex.
I am grateful for passion.
I am grateful for lust.
I am grateful for a sense of humor.
I am grateful for companionship.
I am grateful for my best friend.
I am grateful we communicate well.
I am grateful we love one another.
I am grateful we complement each other.
I am grateful for this opportuni-
ty to share this love with others.

MONEY

I am grateful money flows through me easily.
I am grateful for abundance.
I am grateful for financial freedom.
I am grateful I am able to purchase anything I want.
I am grateful I provide for myself and my family.
I am grateful I donate a lot of money to charity.
I am grateful I am worthy.
I am grateful I am enough.
I am grateful I have no fear or attachments to money.
I am grateful that money is energy.
I am grateful money flows through multiple sources.
I am grateful I am worthy of making a lot of money.
I am grateful I am taken care of.
I am grateful my income increases monthly.
I am grateful I have everything I need.
I am grateful I am living my life's purpose
and that it supports me financially.
I am grateful more money is coming in than going out.
I am grateful I am a money magnet.
I am grateful my bills are paid on time.
I am grateful my bank account is full of extra money.

LIFE'S PURPOSE/CAREER

I am grateful I am living my life's purpose.
I am grateful for the messages and
signs that have led me to
living my purpose.
I am grateful I am living my life's purpose
and that it supports me financially.
I am grateful I am in love with what I do.
I am grateful my life is abundant.
I am grateful I get to shine the light
within me through my work.
I am grateful I am on my path.
I am grateful for love and support.
I am grateful I have a message to share.
I am grateful my skills and inter-
ests are utilized while I work.
I am grateful my work is full of joy.
I am grateful that anything I think, I can create.
I am successful.
I am worthy.
I am enough.
I deserve financial freedom.
I deserve to enjoy life.
I am grateful I am a good human being.
I am grateful for the money that sup-
ports my luxurious lifestyle.

What is your plan for the next thirty days…sixty days? Where do you see your life? What is it you want in life? List five things here you wish to accomplish in the next thirty days and five things for the next sixty days.

Date: _____   Thirty days: _____

1. _____

2. _____

3. _____

4. _____

5. _____

Sixty days: _____

1. _____

2. _____

3. _____

4. _____

5. _____

Made in the USA
Columbia, SC
20 December 2021